Conversations with Saul Bellow
on Esoteric-Spiritual Matters

Conversations
with Saul Bellow
on Esoteric-Spiritual Matters

~ *A Publisher's Recollections* ~

with
Saul Bellow's Foreword to
THE BOUNDARIES OF NATURAL SCIENCE by Rudolf Steiner

Stephen E. Usher

SteinerBooks | 2017

Published by
SteinerBooks | Anthroposophic Press
610 Main Street
Great Barrington, Massachusetts 01230
www.steinerbooks.org

Print ISBN: 978-1-62148-207-9
e-Book ISBN: 978-1-62148-208-6

A version of this work first appeared in Italian with the title "Conversazioni di un editore con Saul Bellow su questioni esoterico spirituali" in *Antroposofia: Rivista Di Scienza Dello Spirito* LXXI, no. 3, 4, & 5 (2016).

The letters to and from Saul Bellow reproduced here are from the personal collection of the author. In Bellow's papers housed at the University of Chicago, this correspondence will be found in Box 77, Folder 13.

Cover photo © Laurence Agron

Printed in the United States of America

Contents

Stephen Usher in the early 1980s

From Liberty Street to Hungry Hollow

A SPRING MORNING IN THE EARLY 1980s found me sitting across the desk from an elegant young woman. At the time I managed the Anthroposophic Press and I was conducting a job interview at our office in the curiously designed Threefold Auditorium in Spring Valley, a west-of-the Hudson River suburb of New York City. My interviewee had responded to a help wanted advertisement. "I've been thinking about the word 'Anthroposophic,'" she said. "'Sophia' means wise and 'anthropos' means person. So this must be the 'wise guy' press." From beyond the grave Rudolf Steiner (1861–1925) must have cracked a smile. He used "anthroposophic" to characterize his ideas, which he memorialized in some 360 German volumes. The Press was busily publishing them in English. Encouraged by this unexpected insight, I dutifully produced Steiner's explanation: Anthroposophy is the bridge from the spirit in the human being to the spirit in the universe. I decided against further clarification with a reference to the bridge in Goethe's *Fairytale of the Green Snake and the Beautiful Lily.* That would be going too

Threefold Auditorim, Spring Valley, New York

far in an interview. But I did offer her a job. It was a disappointment when she turned me down. The highest salary the press could afford was not enough for this capable young person.

This interview was just one of many surprising little experiences that helped me through the tedium of running a small press. That tedium included such activities as writing descriptive blurbs for the hundreds of books in the Press catalogue, tracking our inventory, and overseeing the writing of invoices for the many orders that arrived by mail each day. When the orders were plentiful, I even packed boxes of books. My tiny office, where I did some of this work, opened into the Press bookshop. It was there I had a number of memorable encounters.

In 1980 I had sacrificed my position as a young Ph.D. economist at the Federal Reserve Bank of New York to take on the management of the Anthroposophic Press. My idealism had cost me a pay cut of about 50 percent to say nothing of future income. It had removed me from the stone façade of the New York Fed in lower Manhattan on Liberty Street next to the ill-fated World Trade Center. There I had enjoyed meetings with Paul Volker who, until he became Federal Reserve Chairman, had led the New York Fed. He was a powerful personality. He stood six feet, eight inches tall, and deep voice seemed to boom out of a long tunnel. The room was filled with the smoke of his perpetual cigar. At the Fed I had studied the era's rampant inflation, Bunker Hunt's cornering of the silver market, and other key financial events of the day. But the Anthroposophic Press also had its enticements. It was like patrolling a beach where waves were always washing up some curiosity or other to keep one engaged and interested.

Interesting Encounters

On one occasion three men entered the shop wearing the signature Roman collar of the Catholic priest. They busily selected a large stack of Steiner titles, paid their bill, and departed. I had moved too slowly and missed the opportunity to learn what prompted them to read

Steiner. The opportunity presented itself again when, a few months later, the same three entered the shop. On this occasion I wasted no time coming out of my office. "Are you Catholic priests?" I inquired. Yes, they were. "You appear to read a lot of Steiner," I said. "Yes," they replied, and proceeded freely to tell their tale.

They had been ordained in Spain where they had become interested in Steiner. Their library included a large collection of Steiner in Spanish translation. After some years in a parish in Guatemala, they were transferred to a poor parish within a day's drive of Spring Valley. In transit their Steiner library was lost. Now they were restocking with my English language wares.

"And what do you do with your anthroposophical books," I inquired. "We use them to prepare our sermons. It is the only thing that satisfies the parishioners." This reply was astonishing considering Steiner's works had been on the Catholic Index during the early twentieth century. "How do you square that with your allegiance to the Pope?" I asked. "Our allegiance is to Rudolf Steiner and the Archangel Michael, not the Pope," was their stunning reply.

After these indelible remarks, they paid for a large pile of books and departed. I never saw them again. Another incident that spiced up my life at the Press began with the discovery of a letter in the attic of a house at the Threefold Foundation. To provide some context it is necessary to say a little about the history of the Threefold Foundation.

"Threefold," a Letter and an Idea

Ralph Courtney

Ralph Courtney (1885–1965), a newspaperman of the World War I era who knew Rudolf Steiner personally, established the Foundation. The Foundation property was originally known as "Threefold Farm." Charlotte Parker (1890–1994) purchased it in the early 1920s at a time before a bridge spanned the Hudson River. Ms. Parker, as she was called, was a wealthy member of the St. Mark's Group of the Anthroposophical Society. Members of the group operated a vegetarian restaurant next to Carnegie Hall, in New York City. The farm was purchased as a place for the group to hold its summer conferences and for summer vacations. Over time, a number of anthroposophists built quaint little homes on the property, trying to mimic in miniature the organic architectural style of Rudolf Steiner. Ms. Parker would be asked by one or another member of the group for a spot to build. She would choose a place and there they constructed a house. Eventually a number of these structures became year-round residences.

Threefold Farm in the 1930s

As the twentieth century progressed and bridges spanning the Hudson River were completed, the countryside surrounding the Threefold Farm was transformed from rural farmland to a part of the suburban sprawl of New York City. Ralph Courtney and Ms. Parker looked on these developments as a signal to convert the farm into a foundation dedicated to promoting Steiner's philosophy. Considerable development took place. This included the construction of the Threefold Auditorium, the School of Eurythmy building, and the Green Meadow Waldorf School. Waldorf education for children from kindergarten to twelfth grade is a Steiner innovation popular around the world. Eurythmy, another Steiner innovation, is a movement art.

The main point of this brief history is that odds and ends stored in attics at Threefold could date back to before Steiner's death in 1925, and this was the case with the aforementioned letter that found its way into my hands. It was dated December 16, 1919, and was addressed to Ralph Courtney, who at the time was residing in London, from Rudolf Steiner in Dornach, Switzerland. Dornach was and still is the world head-quarters of Steiner's Anthroposophical Society and the site of his famous building, the Goetheanum.

~

Dornach, December 16th, 1919
Mr. Ralph Courtney, London N. W. 335 Bridge Square
Dear Mr. Courtney!

Let me express my satisfaction at your efforts to get my book The Threefold State† published in English. The same expression of thanks goes to the committee that has been making efforts in this direction.

Enclosed with this letter find a contract with my signature. I am agreeing to the publication of the English edition with this contract. I believe I also shall be able to agree to publication in America.

It is not possible to build an association for the publication of anthroposophical literature in English so long as Mr. Collision has the rights to translate my anthroposophical books into English. Anything that is not

---

† Now available under the title *Towards Social Renewal.*

strictly anthroposophical is not included in those rights. It would be best if The Threefold State were published under the terms of the enclosed contract. Strictly interpreted Mr. Collison held the rights to my anthroposophical books only until 1914. None-the-less conciliatory gestures have to be made for my later purely anthroposophical books—not for The Threefold State—or the situation with Mr. Collison could become awkward. That would delay the publication of The Threefold State.

Determination of the price of the book would be difficult to do from here. The publisher will have to decide that.

I am in agreement with the title: "The Threefold State" and with the subtitle "The True Aspect of the Social Question." The other subtitle does not seem adequate to me.

Now concerning the preface. Mrs. Wedgewood, in particular, says there should not be a preface; and I must say that the grounds for her opinion seem plausible and serious to me. If the publisher wants an introduction to do some good, perhaps the following could be done. Bernard Shaw could write a review of the book that could be printed separately and not as a part of the book. This review could then be placed in each book as a separate insert.

Finally, let me send you a very special Christmas greeting that I also ask you convey to your good mother.

With highest regards,
Yours,
Dr. Rudolf Steiner
Dornach, Switzerland (Canton Soloturn)

Dornach, 16. Dezember 1919
Schweiz.

Mr. Ralph Courtney, London N. W. 3   35 Belsize Square

Lieber Mr. Courtney!

Empfangen Sie den Ausdruck meiner dankenden Befriedigung über Ihre Bemühungen für die englische Veröffentlichung der „Kernpunkte der sozialen Frage". Den gleichen Ausdruck möchte ich auch dem Comité senden, das sich um die Sache so viele Mühe gegeben hat.

Den von mir unterschriebenen Contract lege ich diesem Briefe bei. Ich bin mit dessen Festsetzungen einverstanden. Und ich glaube, dass ich es auch werde sein können mit denen für die Publikation in Amerika.

Es ist nicht möglich zu bilden eine Gesellschaft für Publikation der anthroposophischen Litteratur so lange Mr. Collison das Recht hat, meine eigentlich anthroposophischen Bücher ins Englische zu übersetzen. Alles, was nicht streng anthroposophisch ist, ist nicht in dieses Recht einbezogen. Deshalb werden die „Kernpunkte" am besten in Sinne des mir von Ihnen übersandten Vortrages veröffentlicht. Streng genommen hat Mr. Collison nur das Recht für meine anthrop. Bücher bis 1914. Doch müsste aus consiliantem Entgegenkommen für späteres — mir anthroposophisches, nicht die „Kernpunkte" mit ihm verhandelt werden. Das würde die Publikation der Kernpunkte verzögern.

2.

Die Feststellung des Preises kann ich von hier aus nicht gut beurteilen. Und ich muß das diesbezügliche den Publishers überlassen.

Einverstanden bin ich mit dem Titel: „The Threefold State" und dem Untertitel: „The true Aspect of the Social Problem". Der andre Untertitel scheint mir nicht entsprechend.

Nun bezüglich der Vorrede (preface). Es ist insbesondere Mrs. Wedgewood nicht damit einverstanden, dass jemand zu dem Buche eine Vorrede schreibt; und ich kann mir sagen, das Mrs. Wedgewoods Gründe mir einleuchtend und schwerwiegend erscheinen. Wenn der Publisher will, dass dem Buche doch eine Einführung zu Gute käme, so könnte vielleicht das Folgende gemacht werden. Bernard Shaw könnte eine Recension des Buches schreiben und diese könnte besonders gedruckt werden, ohne auf die Seiten zu Pesen zu kommen, die dem Buche selbst angehören. Die besonderen Blätter könnten dann in jede Copy des Buches eingelegt werden.

Auch ich sende Ihnen herzlichste Weihnachtsgrüße, die ich auch bitte, Ihrer Frau Mutter zu übermitteln.

In vollster Hochachtung

Ihr

Dr. Rudolf Steiner

Dornach, Schweiz (Canton Solothurn).

~

This letter had a peculiar effect on my soul. Chance, I felt, was not the agent that delivered it to my desk. Rather I felt the agent was Rudolf Steiner. Of course, this sounds nuts to a sensible modern ear, but that is how I experienced it. In any case, the letter started my mind in a certain direction, a direction that had real consequences.

Seven years earlier, a literary event lit the horizon of the anthroposophical community. Saul Bellow, the novelist and Nobel Laureate, had published *Humboldt's Gift*, which earned him a Pulitzer Prize. The novel's protagonist studied Steiner's writings with an anthroposophist in Chicago. I wondered: Would Saul Bellow be willing to write a foreword to a translation of one of Steiner's works? The impulse that failed with George Bernard Shaw—I don't know what actually happened but to the best of my knowledge Shaw never wrote a review of *The Threefold State*—might succeed with Bellow.

Katz, DeMay, Bellow

In my pipeline was a translation of Steiner's *Grenzen der Naturerkenntnise*, a series of eight lectures given in the autumn of 1920. It was eventually published in English with the title *The Boundaries of Natural Science,* with a foreword by Saul Bellow. I chose that volume because two of our best translators, both then at Harvard University, were working on it together.

The road to this foreword led through Bellow's novel, *Humboldt's Gift*. Like all the Bellow novels I've read, *Humboldt's Gift* is a first person narrative. The protagonist is Charlie Citrine, and he is clearly modeled on Bellow himself, though, of course, many of the details are fictional. Charlie is a famous writer whose life is in chaos. He is in the middle of a messy divorce. He is in trouble with a petty mob figure. He is involved in a lawsuit. He has girlfriend problems. In the midst of all these distractions, Charlie practices one of Rudolf Steiner's contemplation exercises. He reviews the important details of his biography attempting to remain completely objective and detached. Looming decisively in this biographical landscape is his relation with the late poet Humboldt. Humboldt is modeled on Bellow's real life friend, Delmore Schwartz, a poet who died in 1966.

Occasionally, Charlie visits Dr. Scheldt, an old Anthroposophist, and they discuss Steiner. Charlie summarizes his understanding of certain Steiner passages and Dr. Scheldt elaborates on points that left Charlie uncertain. The figure of Dr. Scheldt was based on a real person, a Chicago anthroposophist named Peter DeMay. Bellow visited him regularly to discuss Steiner.

Dr. Ernst Katz, the University of Michigan physics professor who introduced me to Steiner, knew the real-life Dr. Scheldt and he agreed to introduce me to him.

Peter DeMay was born in Paris in 1901. A mechanical engineer, he worked for a large Chicago firm into his early sixties. After retirement he devoted himself to anthroposophy. A friend described him as a fastidious dresser. Bellow described Dr. Scheldt in words that could have been used for Peter. "He was from another time, entirely. He even dressed like a country club member of the Twenties....I'm speaking to his interested and plain face, calm as a bull's face..."

During the 1970s Peter suffered a heart attack while in a doctor's reception room waiting for a routine appointment. He was out of his body, headed for the afterlife, when he felt a thud on his chest. They were reviving him and it caused terrific pain. In Socratic fashion, he said, "I was never so disappointed in my life. I was about to know everything I had ever wanted to know." He wore a pacemaker after that. The memory of the experience stayed with him, lending a special tone to all his discourses on spiritual matters.

Ernst Katz explained my hope for a Bellow foreword to Peter DeMay. He liked the idea and agreed to a meeting. My contact with Peter started with a phone call. He answered an important question. I had found a number of passages in *Humboldt's Gift* that accurately portrayed aspects of Steiner's thinking. But, after all, *Humboldt's Gift* was fiction. A good writer can create a character who holds a worldview, who articulates it clearly, while the writer does not find it credible. Charlie, the protagonist, also has his doubts. "I'm speaking to his interested and plain face, calm as a bull's face and trying to determine how dependable his intelligence is—i.e., whether we are real here or crazy here." Peter assured me Bellow's interest in Steiner was genuine and serious.

After Peter set up a meeting with Saul Bellow, I flew to Chicago for the appointment. In preparation, I thought a good deal about Bellow and how to approach him. I believe it was my wife Beth, at that time a Eurythmy student, who used the phrase "great soul," to describe him. This felt peculiar at first. People say this of Gandhi or other Eastern spiritual leaders. It hardly seemed to fit to a writer who described rough and tumble life in Chicago. On further reflection I realized it really did apply; he was our American great soul. The content of his soul, expressed in delicious poetic prose, was mirrored in souls by the hundred thousands. He really did illuminate reality in an especially twentieth-century-American kind of way. His editor for *Humboldt's Gift*, Elisabeth Sifton, said this about him in an obituary article:

> I never tried—still don't want—to escape his influence, to lose his incomparable, uproarious, devastating comprehension of the mess we're in. I hear a new joke or learn of some crazy new detail in our national life or meet a new kind of phony, and I need Saul Bellow. Wherever we are, it's somewhere Saul has been before us, and I can't help registering the ways that his

novels transformed ordinary American scenery into radiant loci of intense human meaning. Without him? It can never be.

What makes a great artistic soul what he is? To paraphrase Schiller, the secret art of the master consists of this: he annihilates matter in form. Steiner interprets this in his lectures on *Speech and Drama*. A person can express something directly out of his feelings. That gives rise to ordinary language. An artist recasts this into a form. Then something beyond the original impression is present. The form has overcome the original experience. This is the secret of art. Through the lens of Schiller's idea, Saul Bellow's prose is high art, though it takes a modern perspective to see this.

My mind made up with such ideas, I knocked at the door. It was late in 1981 and I knew I was asking a lot of the Nobel laureate. Thousands of publishers would jump hoops for a Bellow foreword. Success or failure depended, ultimately, on how Saul Bellow felt about Rudolf Steiner and the relation he had with Peter DeMay. I was just an agent. The one thing I couldn't offer was money. The Press's total assets couldn't have exceeded three hundred thousand dollars and the majority of that was tied up in inventory. Bellow probably made that much or more on the royalties of any new book he wrote.

The Boundaries of Natural Science

Saul Bellow turned out to be congenial and unassuming and fascinating. Peter DeMay was very gentle and very wise. A warm friendship was evident between them. Saul's attitude to Rudolf Steiner was clearly one of respect and interest. At the same time there was a healthy questioning and uncertainty.

As I look back on that meeting I don't have a sense for how Saul related to the idea of initiation as Steiner described it. Modern people find the concept baffling. Really, what was the ancient Greek, Herodotus, talking about with the words "mysteries" and "initiation?" Was it just a kooky ceremony where people chanted obscure verses and ran about in silly costumes? A brief sketch of Steiner's explanation goes like this. Our higher being is seed or egg-like. It is capable of transformations whose complexity and purpose are comparable to human embryological development. This development gives birth to a higher man, a supersensible man, who can perceive and function in worlds that are beyond the reach of the ordinary bodily-bound senses. Initiation is the process of this transformation.

In *The Boundaries of Natural Science* Steiner talks about an evolution of the initiation process itself. This is something to try to get the mind around: the process of initiation itself evolves. It changes with developing humanity. The way it was done in oriental antiquity won't work for modern people. *The Boundaries of Natural Science* also differentiates between a path of initiation appropriate for modern people in general and a path specially tailored for people trained in natural science. Two years later, in his foreword, Saul quoted a passage from Rudolf Steiner. He followed it with this language of his own, "I have thought it best not to interpose myself but to allow Steiner to speak for himself, for he is more than a thinker, he is an initiate…"

By the end of our meeting Saul had agreed to a foreword. It was too easy! Probably it had been settled in advance between them.

What turned out to be not-so-easy was Saul actually writing the foreword. He really struggled to complete it and it took him nearly two years. It was serious business for him and he spent a lot of time studying the manuscript. Here was a Nobel author speaking to a scornful century about its own great initiate. I have no doubt that he battled dark forces in soul worlds to carry his experience of Steiner's *Boundaries of Natural Science* through the annihilation process to the sparkling form of his foreword. It is, in itself, a work of art.

Euphoric, I flew back to New York. The Press was humming. The pipeline was full of new titles. Sales were climbing. It would be perfect if I just had enough capital. I had to find money.

Another visit to Chicago

The Press was a not-for-profit organization for good reason. The sale of our literature was never likely to turn a profit. As I applied myself to fundraising, publishing, and marketing, the months went by and not a peep from the Nobel writer. Around June, I took action. Using a sales trip to a big customer, a bookstore on Wabash in Chicago, as an excuse, I flew to the Windy City. Before I left, I called Saul and mentioned I would be in town. We quickly agreed to a visit at his lakeside high-rise condominium on Sheridan Road.

The elevator took me to his floor. Saul welcomed me to his digs and invited me to admire the expansive Lake Michigan view. It was a clear day, the water a beautiful blue blurring into sky. A few ships plied the water of the lake. We talked about the view for a while and then I asked him how the foreword was coming. Yes, he was working on the foreword and studying the manuscript. He was meeting regularly with Peter to discuss Steiner too. We talked about the content of the manuscript and other Steiner ideas. I would just have to be patient; eventually he'd get it done.

During this visit, Saul made some memorable comments on the difficulties of a writer's life. He was complaining. You can't just dive into life like a normal person, he explained. At every moment, part of you is detached; it's observing and taking mental notes and cataloguing the experiences. He said, "As a writer you're handicapped. It's like going through life with one arm tied behind your back."

As I look back on this comment, I realize he was actually describing an essential characteristic of modern consciousness. Steiner points to this essence by saying we live in the era of the "consciousness-soul." This means observer consciousness, detached consciousness. Our era began with the Scientific Revolution about 1400 AD. The leading personalities became relatively more detached from immediate experience than their contemporaries. This allowed them to accurately observe what was going on in the inorganic world, the world of mechanical processes, including mechanical processes in living entities. Galileo watched a swinging church chandelier and measured its movement against his pulse. He constructed an incline plane, then clocked the distance a rolling ball traversed over successive equal time intervals. He discovered gravitational acceleration. The idea of natural law was born.

A picture—or even caricature—of the consciousness-soul is an Englishman, his arms crossed, listening to someone's utter stupidity. He says, "Eh?" with a knowing smile. That's the detached modern soul. From the original pioneers of the scientific revolution the detached observer consciousness spread to ever-widening numbers of people over time. Saul fully embodied this detachment in the best sense of the word and he suffered from it.

In that same year, 1982, Saul Bellow published *The Dean's December*. The book is permeated with the consciousness-soul idea. I have no doubt some of his formulations came from reading Steiner and studying with Peter. The last few pages of the book make this particularly clear. The protagonist, Corde, a university dean, and his astronomer wife, are at Mount Palomar, ascending in the cold to view the stars. He speaks of freedom, penetrating deeper into reality, and the terrible cold.

STILL WAITING...

The months rolled by. Winter was edging up on spring of 1983, and still no foreword. I set out, once again, for Chicago. I rang Saul and mentioned I'd be in town and he invited me to visit at his University of Chicago office. When I arrived he welcomed me in his congenial manner. This time our conversation roamed the landscape of contemporary social issues. Saul was a member of the University's Committee on Social Thought. It was here, a few years later, that he would collaborate with Allan Bloom, writing an introduction to Bloom's famous *The Closing of the American Mind*.

Our conversation often touched the subject of pornography. Saul made observations about the staggering dimensions of the industry. Sales were counted in the billions of dollars. A person didn't need to go to a sleazy move house to see pornography any more, Saul observed. People could imbibe it in the privacy of their homes.

I recently had read about the high incidence of heroin and cocaine use among porn actors in a newspaper article. I added that fact to the mix. The actors needed the money to support their drug habits. Yes, Saul said, they don't feel a thing when they make those films.

We turned to the ideas of Wilhelm Reich. I had read several volumes of Reich's thought. I knew something about this unusual researcher of the human condition. Saul knew more. He had undergone a Reichian analysis in his younger days. The goal of such an analysis is to overcome "body armor," and thus to loosen up and achieve more satisfying sexual orgasms and a better life in general. Saul went through the whole process. At the last session he recalled lying on the couch. He asked the therapist what he should do next. The reply, "Let nature take over." Saul left the session unconvinced. He needed the tensions in his body armor or musculature. He needed his complex set of mental filters. They were part of his personality and of his defense mechanisms.

He needed them to get through life. He wasn't gong to leave it all to nature!

Eventually I brought up the foreword. He assured me he was working at it. But getting his mind around those lectures was not easy. Peter was meeting him regularly.

When our time was up, he offered me a lift. We rode together for a time in his Volvo and continued our conversation. He made a memorable comment. Anthroposophists, he exclaimed, have an easy time of it. He went on to say that they live in a beautiful cocoon, insulated from the real trauma of modern life. They have their own medicines, their biodynamic foods, their Waldorf education. This protects their health and personalities from the disintegration afflicting modern humanity. Moreover, Christianity has been preserved for them by Steiner's spiritual insights. They still have it. For much of the educated Western world it is becoming untenable; the possibility of believing in the divine and an afterlife, much less Christ, has been eaten away by materialistic scholarship.

I had to admit there was some validity to his analysis. But his view of the rosy life of anthroposophists was, I felt, a bit too rosy.

SPLENDID ISOLATION?

In a way, Bellow's criticism paralleled one Steiner artic-
ulated in a series of important lectures given in 1913–
14, published in English as *The Fifth Gospel*. Using his
initiate faculties, Steiner found his way in occult vision
back to the time of Jesus. In the lectures, he reports specific details that are visible in the supersensible traces of
history, known as the Akashic Record. Steiner explains
the nature of the Akasha in his book, *Cosmic Memory*.

The concept of the Akashic Record has caused considerable confusion. I am told that an Anthroposophical
Society library once received a letter from a minister requesting to borrow the Akashic Record. It was
explained to him that the Akashic Record was not
something a library could lend because the Record was
actually part of the etheric world. The minister wrote
back in a huff saying, "I always knew you people were
secretive!"

One detail reported in *The Fifth Gospel* lectures
concerns the relation of Jesus to the Essene community
prior to the Baptism. The Essenes, according to Steiner,
possessed a deep knowledge of spiritual realities. Their
community life was organized to allow spiritual insights
to grow among them. To this end, they lived ascetic
lives, followed strict dietary rules, and organized their
days to accord regular time for spiritual practices. A

new member, upon joining the community, transferred all his wealth to it. The individual Essene no longer was encumbered by the distraction of personal material possessions.

Living in this fashion, the Essenes made steady spiritual progress. As members advanced, older brethren imparted certain secrets. These were strictly guarded. Jesus, though not an Essene, was always welcome in the Essene communities. They recognized his spiritual stature and spoke freely about matters normally reserved for advanced members of the community.

In his late twenties, Jesus came to realize something that caused him great sorrow. He recognized that the Essenes purchased their spiritual advancement at the expense of other human beings. The pure Essene life made it impossible for certain harmful spirits to approach Essene communities. With supersensible sight, Jesus saw these spirits running from the gates of an Essene village. He knew they were running to other human communities. They attacked the inhabitants of the other communities all the more. Jesus was seeking a road that all people could travel to the spirit, so he rejected the Essene life, which could save only the few.

Saul's criticism of anthroposophists was a bit like saying they had created an Essene-like environment to shelter themselves from the world. With my knowledge of anthroposophists I felt this was an exaggeration.

Some of them would, no doubt, like to live in such splendid isolation, but modern life simply will not accommodate this. It finds you out no matter where you hide.

Naturally, materialists will deny the possibility of a science of the spirit. It follows that they also will reject findings like those concerning Jesus among the Essenes. In November of 1983, I talked with Saul about this problem by phone. An experience he mentioned illustrated the situation. He once debated with a mathematician and with a Kantian philosopher. The Kantian refused to discuss Steiner, would not even explain his objections. The mathematician followed suit. Saul said, "They won't even give their arguments against him, so you can't know." In our time, Saul felt, academics control what is regarded as credible. Their strategy with Steiner is to ignore him.

AN ARRIVAL AND A DEPARTURE

Several months after my Chicago visit, an envelope arrived with Saul's return address. It was the foreword! My expectations were surpassed. I rushed the manuscript through the production steps and prepared a press release.

Before books arrived from the printer, a sad event occurred. Peter DeMay died on September 9, 1983.

Neither the foreword nor Saul's great novel, *Humboldt's Gift*, could have happened without him. He was the teacher who could interpret Steiner for Saul Bellow. Peter crossed the threshold as soon as Saul had completed the task. He didn't even wait around to get his complimentary copy.

By phone, Saul and I discussed Peter's crossing. We attempted Steiner's exercise for communicating with the dead. Steiner offered this advice for putting a question to a deceased loved one. Picture him, as vividly as possible, in the evening just before going to sleep. Think of things you did together. Recall the timbre of his voice. Then imagine *him* asking *you* the question you want to ask him. If I wanted to ask Peter whether the after death scene was what he had expected, I'd visualize him saying to me, "Do I find the after-death world as I expected it to be?"

To receive the answer, Steiner explained, you had to be very attentive just as you awoke in the morning. It was best to awaken naturally, without the aid of an alarm clock, because that is an immediate distraction. If you succeed, an inner picture will arise in you, a picture of yourself answering the question. In other words, you see and hear yourself giving an answer. What you hear is actually your dead friend's answer to your question. I might have heard myself saying, "I entertained the correct concept of the afterlife while I was alive. But the experience is a bit like a person who heard about elephants, though he never saw an elephant or even a picture of one. Sighting an actual elephant would still be shocking. Similarly I'm shocked about the afterlife."

According to Steiner, then, the ideal is to fall asleep picturing your dead friend asking the question. Upon awakening you see yourself answering. To my experience, the answers can also come in a weaker way. Thoughts emerge in my consciousness during the day. Sometimes it is obvious these are not my thoughts, but whisperings from a friend across the threshold. When the answer comes this way, however, it leaves an uncertainty about the source.

~

Saul told me that he was worried about Peter. Peter, he said, had a pretty fixed idea about the afterlife. Saul feared Peter was having a hard time because it wasn't as he had expected. I felt Saul had actually managed to find his way empathetically to Peter's soul and he experienced Peter wrestling with the elephant problem.

Steiner's method for communicating with those on the other side hints about the nature of the other world. On yonder side, things are turned inside out. What here is outside is inside there, and vise versa. That means all human and superhuman beings are experienced as having their existence inside of us. We occupy the same place. Communicating over there can be compared to experiencing thoughts welling up from within on this side. The challenge is sorting out the identity of what is welling up. Suddenly, you have a world inside of you, but you are accustomed to having only you in you. What exactly *are* you under such circumstances? How do you relate to all the others occupying the same inside? Was this the problem Peter was facing?

I was sorry Peter had gone so quickly. If he had waited around just a little longer he would have enjoyed hearing of the many periodicals that reviewed *The Boundaries of Natural Science*. A consequence of the foreword and the resulting reviews was increased sales of the book. Orders from individual buyers and bookstores were above normal. More significant were the large number of library orders.

When Peter crossed the Styx, Saul missed the conversation. He participated, once, in the Chicago Steiner group. The occasion was not exactly a memorable one. No one could take Peter's place. His was a rare spiritual maturity. He was in the big leagues like my wonderful Dornach mentors and Ernst Katz. But Saul didn't have a relationship with any of them.

The challenge to awake

I talked anthroposophical ideas with Saul anytime I could manage a visit. But I didn't manage often. On one visit—probably in May of 1984—we wrestled with themes Saul had tackled in *Humboldt's Gift*. They appear in the second half of the novel. The relevant passage begins, "What did give me great comfort was to talk with Dr. Scheldt." The next pages discuss some of Steiner's ideas. Saul starts by comparing Rip van Winkle's twenty-year nap to modern society's inability to wake up to spiritual reality.

There is nothing vague or abstract about Steiner's idea of awakening spiritually. Getting specific about spiritual reality—specific like a description of how a carburetor or a fuel injection system works—is not acceptable in polite company. It is strictly forbidden by the high priests who call the shots at modern universities. Steiner is very specific in *The Work of the Angels in Man's Astral Body*, one of the works Saul wrote about in *Humboldt's Gift* and later in *More Die of Heartbreak*. Shock at the detailed descriptions is a hurdle the prospective reader has to surmount.

The astral body is visible to a developed clairvoyant, and what is seen is sometimes called an aura. It extends beyond the etheric body. Any creature that experiences pleasure and pain must have an astral body.

It is the vehicle that gives rise to sensation. The human astral body is about twice the height and four times the width of the physical body. To clairvoyant sight, it is a constantly moving and undulating body of color qualities. To give just a taste of Steiner's detailed descriptions, consider these points from his *Spiritual Research: Methods and Results*. People who largely follow animal instincts have very different astral bodies than those who spend much time thinking. Those exhibiting emotional outbursts arising from their animal nature have auras of largely red and brown hues. People who mix cunning with their emotions show red mixed with green. A thinking person has an aura exhibiting a pleasant shade of green. This is particularly true of people "never at a loss in life." Devotional types develop blue shades in their auras. These are good souls who have little thought power. If these good souls are also intelligent, then green currents intermingle with the blue shades. Inventive people with fruitful ideas radiate light colors from a "particular point within." People who are affected strongly by outside impressions exhibit a continual flaring up of red spots in the aura. Bluish spots with an unstable form indicate a scattered person. This is just a hint of Steiner's extensive description. In *The Work of the Angels in Man's Astral Body*, he explores even deeper aspects of the human astral body.

A key idea expressed there is that angels are etching certain designs or pictures into contemporary human astral bodies. This intrigued Saul. The designs indicate the path human evolution should follow. But whether that happens depends on human beings. Since the fifteenth century, the dawning of the era of the consciousness-soul, humans have reached cosmic maturity and have choices to make.

Steiner calls one of these designs "an impulse of brotherhood." An intense interest in other people will arise if the design is accepted by humanity. It won't be a leisurely experience. With a sudden jolt, we will recognize what the other man or woman actually is. This will lead to heightened empathy. The result: a happy person won't be at peace if his neighbors are suffering. I suspect Saul was familiar with these jolts. They brought flashes of insight that found their way into the characters in his novels.

Another angelic picture reveals the hidden divinity in each fellow human. A third gives insight into the spiritual nature of the world and confidence that the spiritual can be reached by thinking. This third picture indicates how the power of thought will attain the ability to cross an abyss and experience spiritual reality.

These angelic pictures challenge humanity to wake up, to leave the Rip van Winkle slumber. Waking up requires inner exertion. If we make the effort, we can become aware of the angelic pictures, which will then lead humanity in the intended direction.

If people opt for slumber, the angel's work becomes a game. But the angels are in earnest and won't accept this. If we keep on snoring, the angels will be forced to move their activity one level down. That means they would elaborate their pictures in sleeping etheric bodies. Then results would follow without human cooperation. If that happens, the possibility of becoming aware of these pictures will be lost entirely. Instead of leading in the direction the angels intended, the angelic impulses would have to work into human instincts. The outcome would be a terrible caricature of the divine design.

Saul and I discussed these caricatures and we looked for signs of them in contemporary civilization. Our conversation centered on the sexual aberrations Steiner predicted. If Rip continued to sleep, the angels would instill certain sexual instincts in sleeping humans. The result: men would become "half devil." The sexual life, said Steiner, would "arise in a pernicious form, instead of wholesomely, in clear waking consciousness." What would arise would not be considered an aberration either. Instead it would become an accepted part of social life. Scientists would label it natural behavior. Something would enter the blood, explained Steiner, "as the effect of sexual life." It would eliminate brotherly feelings among men. Social Darwinism would be triumphant.

Medicine was another area where new instinctive knowledge would arise. Steiner predicted that medical science would make "giant leaps." Substances and therapies would be discovered that provide pleasurable experiences. In actuality they would make patients ill but this would be ignored. Confusion about the very meaning of health and illness would be rampant.

Failure to see the angel's pictures would also give rise to what Steiner called an instinct for mechanical occultism. This was the third caricature that Saul and I discussed. This instinct would lead to the discovery of a new source of energy. It would "unleash a tremendous mechanical force in the world."

The growth of the pornography industry in relation to home video was one piece of evidence to which Saul pointed. It might well be an initial manifestation of the sexual aberrations. (Internet porn would not arrive for another decade.) He also talked about other aspects of the sexual revolution. Some of these were elaborated further, a few years later, in *More Die of Heartbreak.* "Denied access to the soul, the angels work directly on the sleeping body. In the physical body this angelic love is corrupted into human carnality. Such is the source of all the disturbed sexuality of the present age." In *More Die of Heartbreak,* Saul attributed these ideas to a fictitious character named Yermelov, while he named Steiner as the source in *Humboldt's Gift.*

Why didn't he mention Steiner? My guess is he worried mentioning Steiner might turn off some of his readers. That would have financial consequences he couldn't afford.

Health, illness, "mechanical occultism"

When we discussed Steiner's idea about "feel good" medicine we speculated that anxiety disorder medications like Librium and Valium might be examples. Prozac for depression and panic disorders hadn't yet arrived, nor had panic attacks for that matter. We also didn't know about Viagra, which really hits the mark. Old people risk their health to experience sexual pleasure in their golden years. Of course, if you view yourself as meat on the bone destined for extinction, the risk could appear rational. But for anyone who knows about the life between death and rebirth and about reincarnation and karma, Viagra is folly. Old age offers an opportunity to live free of intense instincts. That makes it easier to explore spiritual reality. Such exploration prepares us for the great journey into the ocean of soul and spirit that commences upon dying.

Mechanical occultism is what Keeley[†] discovered. It was puzzling to me that Steiner gave this force such a negative connotation in *The Work of the Angel*. He spoke of it in a more positive light elsewhere. He does make clear that its premature introduction into civilization could spell disaster. It will only be a boon if civilization has accepted certain spiritual realities as fact before some inventor discovers mechanical occultism. Steiner claims an instinctive search for this force would arise in humans who failed to wake up to the angels' activity. But Steiner encouraged his pupil Ehrenfried Pfeiffer to conduct experiments that might have led to the discovery of this energy. He was not successful, but it seems to follow that Steiner felt mechanical occultism could be found by fully conscious means.

As evidence of the search for this energy we spoke about Joseph Newman. In the 1980s, Newman published an article claiming he had found a Keeley-like energy. I had discussed this article with Georg Unger and I explained what I had learned to Saul.

Saul brought Wilhelm Reich into the conversation too. Reich had ideas about what constituted healthy sexuality. Did his ideas shed light on what Steiner meant by sexual aberrations? I was uneasy about Reich and worried that his ideas led in an unhealthy direction. Saul did not share my concern.

---

†   John Ernst Worrell Keely (1827–1898), American inventor

During our conversation I tried to recall some other Steiner texts related to *Work of the Angels*. But my recall was sketchy. It was embarrassing given Saul's amazing memory. I did remember that Steiner had spoken in one lecture of three "occultisms." He labeled them mechanical, hygienic, and eugenic. In another place, he explained that a kind of revolution was happening in the world of the angels. They were being split into two different groups based on the behavior of the humans to whom they were linked. The idea of pairing angels and humans is similar to the notion of guardian angels. Steiner was saying the guardian angel's destiny depended on whether their human woke up spiritually or chose to orient his mind based exclusively on materialistic conceptions. Angels whose humans opened the atrium of their minds to spiritual considerations underwent a development of their own. This lifted these angels into higher spiritual spheres. The other angels, attached to humans who kept the atrium closed, descended into lower regions.

When I arrived back in Spring Valley I carefully re-read the two texts I had recalled imperfectly and summarized my findings in a letter to Saul.

~

June 6, 1984

Dear Saul,

After our Chicago conversation I decided to look a little deeper into, "Work of the Angels" etc. This ultimately prodded my memory, which performs like an old mule, into coughing up some connections. Specifically I started to compare the above with two other lectures. One is, "Entry of the Michael Forces; Decisive Character of the Michael Impulse." It is among the lectures in Karmic Relationships *Vol. III and was given on Aug. 3, 1924. The other is, "Mechanistic, Eugenic, and Hygenic Aspects of the Future." You will find it in our volume* Challenge of the Times. *It was delivered on Dec. 1, 1918 about two months after "Work of the Angels."*

Taken together these lectures make concrete, awfully concrete, what Steiner means when he describes ours as a time of transition. The lecture of 1924 links human and angelic activity with that of Michael [the Archangel] since 1879, the year he assumed the role of Time Spirit. The Michael force operating at a spiritual level in contradistinction to the Gabrielic is calling men to a new level of noetic exertion. Through freedom men are to find their way to thinking about the spiritual. The idea is explained by analogy in The Case for Anthroposophy. *You may recall Barfield's introduction. He pictures two relatives going their separate ways. One concerns himself only with material reality and accomplishes the development of science and technology. The other, to whom the call is addressed, is to concern himself with purely spiritual activity independent of the material. This will make possible the development of a science of the spirit.*

The entry of the Michael Forces marks the end of a period where moral and natural law are separated. Those human beings who in freedom develop thoughts about the purely spiritual, exercise a force which severs them from racial and national characteristics. The effect of this exertion will reach to the physiognomy in the next incarnation. These individuals will be born all over the globe and appear as not belonging to any racial or national group, their physiognomy reflecting instead their true individuality (what you might call a personal style!) The effect extends into the realm of the angels. Angels connected with human beings who take up spiritual thoughts will undergo a different evolution than those connected with men who choose not to do so. The spiritual forces exercised in one life effect the natural forms of the next and the development of higher beings.

The time of transition is thus one of shattering separations. The human and angelic worlds are divided. Two groups are formed. "While the Michael community is being formed here upon earth, we behold above it the ascending and the descending angeloi. Looking more deeply into the world today, one can perpetually observe these streams, which are such as to stir the heart to its foundations." He goes into some detail about the difficult karma of those entering the Michael community. By destiny they are connected with human beings who cannot or will not take up the spiritual activity. Thus deep karmic ties must be dissolved as one soul takes the ascending path while the other takes the descending one.

"The Work of the Angels," is essentially an elaboration of the relationship between the human and angelic beings. It shows the difference between the case where men take up

the noetic exertion and the case where they fail to do so. Where the activity is taken up the individual emerges. He has access to the spiritual world through thinking. Through inspiration he can grasp the spiritual nature of other men giving him a genuine interest in them and making possible a true brotherhood. By grasping the spiritual core of the other and seeing it as an image of the godhead a true freedom of religion can emerge. Where the exertion is not made the angel must work directly into the etheric. Then certain elemental properties arise from human nature which in "Work of the Angels" Steiner describes as "baleful."

In "The Mechanistic, Eugenic, and Hygenic Aspects of the Future," Steiner describes essentially the same properties arising from the elemental nature of men but fails to label them baleful. In fact he does not even suggest there is an alternative nor does he mention the angels. Here these qualities are characterized as innate capacities of different peoples. Mechanical occultism will arise instinctively in the peoples of the West. From the East a special ability for eugenics will emerge. The middle will be gifted with certain elemental capacities of healing. All of this is pictured as emerging from the people or folk and not the individual. Moreover, the peoples of the different regions will be able to acquire the abilities of the other regions through association and cooperation. The lecture continues with a sort of occult analysis of geo-politics. Essentially the lodges of England and America alone are aware of these innate capacities. This knowledge is being used to gain power over the other parts of the world.

The picture that emerges is quite interesting. When men fail to take up in freedom the individual path to the *spirit instinctive forces emerge in peoples. These forces then determine the future evolution of these peoples. How it will stand for those who become individualized is not discussed in this lecture, but Steiner does make reference to this in other places.*

Turing to Reich, I would make a few conjectures from the little I know of him. First his orgone energy seems to be a step toward mechanical occultism. Second his struggles with issues of personality and sexuality place him in the middle of the polarity of brotherhood and sexual aberrations. The enclosed article from his early writings is quite revealing. His discussion of "sexual aura" etc. certainly leads in the direction of being interested only in the instinctive side of human nature. If consciousness is directed largely to this aspect of others we will indeed become half animals behaving like dogs around bitches in heat. The other pole is an interest in the spiritual core of others, the true individuality. An important question is whether an interest in the true individuality can emerge with sufficient energy to actually dominate the instinctive forces.

To conclude I should mention that there is evidence regarding the American instinct for mechanical occultism. Hundreds of patent applications are submitted each year for perpetual motion machines. Such a machine is considered impossible by science as it violates laws of thermodynamics. Steiner suggests that the thing is possible when the etheric world is added to the physical. Needless to say, a machine which could produce more energy than it used would make energy essentially a free good and give those who controlled it tremendous power. Enclosed is an article from Science

(Newman's Impossible Motor). The next time we meet I will tell you about my phone conversation with Joe Newman.

> *With Warm Regards,*
> *Steve Usher*

> *P.S. I loved your last book!*

Here is Saul's reply:

> *Box 314D Rte 4 West Brattleboro, Vt 05301*
> *6.28.84*

Dear Steve:

Your letter with its resume—so succinct and thorough: excellent!—is very useful to me, will save me any amount of digging and puzzling. The keenness of some of Steiner's forecasts has no parallel. Others leave me stranded. About the English-speaking peoples, for instance, he seems entirely in the right. They are aggressively, if not angrily, "doing right", are lopsidedly beneficial in intent with their science and democracy. An instructive pamphlet might be written on Steiner's view of the Americans. Even an anthology of his statements on Woodrow Wilson would be worth poring over. I can assimilate the prediction that a special ability for eugenics will emerge from the East, but that the people of the center will, as a folk, manifest capacities for healing forces me to apply the measure of Nazi Germany to Steiner's prediction. The best I can do with that is to postpone judgment, keep an open mind. (Open = skeptical).

The term "mechanical occultism" is correct for W. Reich. Curiously, however Reich is not without spiritual interests.

The human being as Reich sees him is and is not an animal. He is sick because he has lost his animal nature, but this is in some degree a human and not an animal sickness. It is only in health that the human being is capable of being moral, capable moreover of loving. Neurotic man has no spiritual life, cannot have one. Spirit of course takes its source in Nature, and Reich is satisfied here to make great gestures towards the God of Nature, a Scientific God. He abhors "mysticism", which he reads as sexually inspired deformity.

Many thanks for your letter and the Xeroxes,
Saul

~

FURTHER CONVERSATIONS

In 1986 and 1987 I visited Saul several times at his Vermont home. It was a traditional New England house with white clapboard siding in a country setting with a lovely yard. It was a generous house with high ceilings and plenty of floor space.

Saul received me in the front rooms. I was there to talk anthroposophy with him. These conversations fascinated me. The way Saul formulated things always gave me new insights. I felt privileged to have private talks with a guy who had the "magics." Several hundred thousand people wanted to read whatever he wrote. I hoped he would write more about Steiner. I was, and remain, convinced that the fate of civilization depends on people waking up to Steiner. In a veiled way a lot of Steiner had found its way into *The Dean's December*. Ph.D. dissertations could be written on that theme.

During one of my visits, Saul was writing *More Die of Heartbreak*. He had just laid down his pen when I rang the doorbell. On the writing table I saw a stack of yellow, legal sized pads. They were bound together with a rubber band. The one on top was half filled. His method, it seemed, was to fill a pad and then place it at the bottom of the stack.

I asked him what it was like when he was in the process of writing. He told me it was like being high. All kinds of thoughts were weaving in his consciousness and he was highly concentrated. I had the impression that he wrote quite rapidly when he got going. He seemed pretty charged when I entered.

Another thought came to my mind as we discussed his creative process. I had read somewhere about a person who claimed he was Bellow's model for the protagonist in *Henderson the Rain King*. Saul admitted that he borrowed some characteristics from this fellow. But Henderson, in his totality, was really quite different. Saul continued with this observation. Many people are desperately searching for identity and latch onto whatever they can find. This is how Saul saw the fellow that claimed to be the Henderson model. Saul took a few traits from him and the man identified with the fictional character.

This led me to another obvious question. Would any of my characteristics show up in *More Die of Heartbreak?* He said it was inevitable! This alarmed me. Apparently anybody and anything around him while he wrote was subject to being milked for useful characteristics. When I finally saw the published book, I discovered Saul had included a disclaimer. The book made no reference to any living person though portions of the novel were derived from real facts. The same disclaimer appeared in *The Dean's December.* When I read *More Die of Heartbreak* I could see plainly how Saul picked up aspects of our interaction and wove them into his tale.

Another topic we explored was sex and love. We talked about the pain of separation and divorce. Saul assured me he knew that pain all too well. He had separated from four wives. Out of my lower nature I said something like, "Well it's all about getting laid, isn't it!" Saul scolded me saying, "You know it is much more than that." I was ashamed for allowing my lower nature to speak in that manner. Of course I knew in my higher self that there was far more than that to human relations between men and women. Deep oceanic longings are involved that are hard to fathom.

People suffer from these longings. It usually

remains unconscious or semiconscious. But they look to satisfy it through a lover or spouse. They are struggling to satisfy something that a partner probably can't satisfy. In *More Die of Heartbreak* Saul wrote, "What it comes down to is that men and women are determined to get out of one another (or tear out) what is simply not to be gotten by any means."

Longing was just one topic Saul and I discussed in Vermont. I also had a conversation with him about the artistic quality of Steiner's works. Saul felt that many Steiner passages were world-class literature with a style and beauty all their own. We even discussed publishing a book of such passages and I tried to persuade Saul to make the selection; but it never happened. Another topic was Steiner's claim about higher states of consciousness, the consciousness that awakens when the chakras are turning. We talked about our inability directly to perceive most of the things Steiner described. We could only know them as ideas, not as direct inner perception. Then Saul said something I never will forget. "But we must know!" He spoke this with emotional intensity. His soul longed to see through the great riddles of human existence. Understanding what Steiner saw, being able to think the thoughts he formed about his experiences was a tremendous help. Yet it was not a substitute for actually beholding what Steiner claimed to have seen.

In a way Saul worked with the idea of spiritual sight in *More Die of Heartbreak*. The novel's protagonist, Benn Carter, is a plant biologist, even a "plant clairvoyant." He has a special talent for penetrating the plant kingdom, which is to say the realm of life.

According to Steiner, in *Theosophy* to mention one source, the realm of life is that higher world nearest to the kingdom of dead nature. Normal waking consciousness today is suited for understanding the dead world only. This consciousness can discover natural laws. Using those laws it can invent new technologies. But our normal waking consciousness is not suited to understand life. The tremendous progress in genetics and the associated technology are really discoveries and manipulations of the dead parts of living things. Our science is penetrating ever deeper into the mechanical parts of living beings but not into life itself. For example, no one understands why a broken bone grows back together. The real power of life still eludes human understanding.

To step from the realm of dead systems into the realm of life requires a higher stage of consciousness. Steiner describes several levels of consciousness lying above our normal waking state. The esoteric student who achieves certain steps in his development can make use of these higher stages of consciousness. The first Steiner calls "Imaginative" consciousness. The choice of the term can be understood this way. The esoteric student must meditate on certain pictures and images to develop his sight. The pictures must not, however, be invented by the student. He must obtain them from an initiate. This can be done by way of a book like *Knowledge of the Higher Worlds and Its Attainment.* The student then creates these received pictures with his active fantasy or imagination. He holds them in his mind to the exclusion of all other mental content for a certain amount of time each day. This effort places something in his astral body that does not dissolve during the night the way normal mental content dissolves. Instead the images persist and begin to form the chakras. The first realm entered by the use of the chakras is called, in Steiner's language, the Imaginative world. One experiences it using Imaginative consciousness.

Imaginative consciousness gives the spiritual scientist the possibility of really understanding living things. In particular it gives the capacity to understand the realm of plants. As I mentioned above, Benn Carter, the protagonist in *More Die of Heartbreak,* is a "plant clairvoyant." In the novel Benn's life proceeds nicely as long as he sticks with the world of plants. But he gets into trouble when he tries to deal with his own longings and the world of his sexual desires and instincts.

The novel tells the story of Benn's mounting troubles as he tries to satisfy his longings. The crisis point arrives when he realizes his entanglements in the desire-world have destroyed his plant clairvoyance. He had recently married a young, beautiful woman. She is a schemer with plans for Benn. He finds himself living in his in-laws' ritzy apartment. It slowly dawns on Benn that marrying was a terrible mistake. To console himself when life get difficult with his wife and in-laws he communes with an azalea plant in his mother-in-law's study. The study is off-limits to Benn, so the communion takes place at a distance. He gazes furtively at the azalea through the study door. Near the end of the novel Benn sneaks into the study to be closer to the azalea. He makes a shattering discovery: the plant is artificial!

He lost his plant clairvoyance. He can no longer sense life. Learning to distinguish between living and dead objects is among the first esoteric exercises in Steiner's *Knowledge of the Higher Worlds and Its Attainment*. The student is directed to turn his attention to budding, growing, flourishing life on the one hand, and to phenomena connected with fading, decaying, and withering on the other. The exercise can be practiced effectively by comparing plant buds to shed leaves that are withering. By following the steps of the exercise the student learns to recognize polar signature feelings that lawfully accompany these polar phenomena. Steiner compares the signature feeling of burgeoning life to the feelings that accompany a sunrise. The feeling that accompanies the slowly rising moon is similar to withering and decaying. When the student has achieved the ability to clearly experience these signature feelings he has taken a basic step on the path of esoteric training. He has graduated from kindergarten to first grade for spiritual scientists.

Not to miss the point here, it is important to understand that these feelings arise in the soul in the same way that the colors red or blue arise in consciousness if a person has healthily functioning eyes. It is also essential to get beyond a fundamental error that haunts modern civilization. The philosopher Kant introduced this error into human thinking. The person possessed by this error says, in a nutshell, "How do I know that what I see as blue is not what you see when you see red?" If you think this way you naturally believe that colors and all feelings are subjective. Steiner shows the error in this way of thinking in his seminal work *The Philosophy of Spiritual Activity*.

Benn Carter was a master of the living-dying exercise and then lost his mastery. Saul wove the whole riddle of human passions and desires into his tale. These must be brought into a state of calmness before the soul can become aware of signature feelings and the many spiritual experiences beyond those basic ones. Swirling passions muddy the soul's waters. They are like loud muzak blotting out a bird's song.

~

I never saw Saul again. At the end of 1988, I left the Anthroposophic Press to take a job with an economic consulting firm that engaged in litigation support. That took me to Terrytown, New York, a suburb of New York City where I lived from 1988 to 2001. I followed Saul's career and read his new books. Occasionally we exchanged greetings by mail. Here is a note he sent me in July of 1990:

> *Dear Steve,*
>
> *I answer your November letter in July. Being behind the times by eight months is not too terrible. I can always blame it on lunar cycles. I was a little startled to hear that you left the Press, but I can easily understand that it was a difficult position and readily imagine that you would have a regiment of detractors and fussy quarterbacks from the organization to bug you. You'll be happier bringing malefactors of great wealth (FDR's phrase) to justice …*
>
> *Saul*

~

In 2000, Saul's *Ravelstein* appeared. I read it with consuming interest. The protagonist, Chick, describes how his dead friend, Ravelstein, entered his consciousness. The description rang true to my own experience. "He had a strange way of turning up. … He came in obliquely from wherever it was he continued to exist."

Saul also defended his talking about such experiences. "I can't sit on information simply because it's not intellectually respectable information."

During my days as a consultant I enjoyed reading Saul's novels and some of Steiner's books, but I didn't have a lot of time for spiritual matters. My time and energy were focused on business. It was an exhilarating time and I learned a tremendous amount during those years about practical matters. I did manage to reserve a small corner of my life for Steiner interests by leading a Steiner study group with the help of Beth, my lovely wife. We called it the "Jupiter Group," after the star of Thursday, the day of our weekly evening meetings. The group usually met in our apartment. Over the years some eighty people participated in Jupiter Group studies.

In 1999 I left the consulting firm to start my own practice. Then in January 2001 Beth and I moved to a beautiful home in the Adirondack Mountains. We enjoyed the bucolic setting and the silent forest for several years. Then the 35°-below-zero winters started wearing on me so we moved southwest, down to Texas, which was sort of out-of-the-freezing pan and into the Texas heat. So I became a Texan. I'm also a "wise guy" in the sense bestowed on the term by the young lady I interviewed at the Anthroposophic Press. As I reported at the beginning of this narrative, she explained it like this. Sophia means wisdom. "Anthropos" means person or guy. So an Anthroposophist is a wise guy. That makes me a Texas wise guy!

Here in Texas I started caring for bees. I have two hives of friendly Russian bees. Steiner talks about bees in his Nine Lectures on *Bees*. He tells that the hive is, in a certain way, a very advanced life form. Their social organization, taken to a higher level, is a harbinger of the future.

~

Saul crossed the river Styx in the same year I moved to Texas. Since then he has become one of "my dead," to use his own expression. He regularly pops into my consciousness and sometimes I hold a kind of inner conversation with him. To conclude the American edition of this short work—it first appeared in an Italian Anthroposophical Journal—I put a question to Saul in my evening meditation by imagining him asking me this question: "Steve, is there any thought I should like to communicate to end this work?" What came to me the next morning was this thought: "I am glad to have helped Rudolf Steiner become better known."

Saul Bellow's Foreword
to
The Boundaries of Natural Science (1983)

Rudolf Steiner in 1916

THE AUDIENCE ATTENDING THIS SERIES of lectures in 1920 was at once informed by Rudolf Steiner that he proposed to consider the connections between natural science and social renewal.

Everyone agrees, he says, that such a renewal requires a renewal of our thinking (one must remember that he was speaking of the groping and soul-searching that followed the great and terrible war of 1914–18), yet not everyone "imagines something clear and distinct when speaking in this way."

Steiner then sketches rapidly the effects of the scientific world-view on the modern social order. Scientific progress has made us very confident of our analytical powers. Inanimate nature, we are educated to believe, will eventually become transparently intelligible. It will yield all its secrets under scientific examination, and we will be able to describe it with mathematical lucidity. After we have conquered the inorganic we will proceed to master the organic world by the same means.

The path of scientific progress however has not been uniformly smooth. Steiner reminds us that by the end of the 19th century doubts concerning the origins of scientific knowledge had arisen within the scientific community itself, and in a famous and controversial lecture the physiologist du Bois-Reymond asked the question, How does consciousness arise out of material processes? What is the source of the consciousness with which we examine the outer world? To this du Bois-Reymond answers, *Ignorabimus*—we shall never know.

In this *Ignorabimus* Steiner finds a parallel to an earlier development, that of medieval Scholasticism. Scholastic thinking had made its way to the limits of the super-sensible world. Modern natural science has also reached a limit. This limit is delineated by two concepts: "matter"—which is everywhere assumed to be within the sensory realm but nowhere actually to be found — and consciousness, which is assumed to originate within the same world, "although no one can comprehend how." Can we fathom the fact of consciousness with explanations conceived in observing external nature? Steiner argues that we cannot. He suggests that scientific research is entangling itself in a web, and that only outside this web can we find the real world. The great victories of science have subdued our minds. We accept the all pervading scientific method. It has transformed the earth. Nevertheless it seems incapable of understanding its own deepest sources. Scientific method as we of the modern world define it can bring us only to the *Ignorabimus* because it is powerless to explain the consciousness that directs it. In our study of nature, and by means of our concept of matter, we have made everything very clear, but this clarity does not give us Man. Him we have lost. And the lucidity to which we owe our great successes in the study of the external world is rejected by consciousness itself. For in the depths of consciousness there lies a will, and this will revolts when lucid science tries to "think" Man as it thinks external nature.

To conclude from this that Steiner is "anti-science" would be a great mistake. To him science is a necessary, indeed indispensable stage in the development of the human spirit. The scientific examination of the external world awakens consciousness to clear concepts and it is by means of clear conceptual thinking that we become fully human. Spiritual development requires a full understanding of pure thought, and pure thought is thought devoid of sensory impressions. "Countless philosophers have expounded the view that pure thinking does not exist, but is bound to contain traces, however diluted, of sense perception. A strong impression is left that philosophers who maintain this have never really studied mathematics, or gone into the difference between analytical and empirical physics," Steiner writes. Mathematical thought is thought detached from the sense world, and as it is entirely based upon rules of reason that are universal it offers spiritual communion to mankind, as well as a union with reality. It is moreover a *free* activity. Spiritual training, says Steiner, reveals it to be not only sense-free but also brain-free. The operations of thought are directed by spiritual powers. Pure thinking leads to the discovery of freedom and leads us to the realm of spirit. And Steiner tells us explicitly that out of sense-free thinking "there can flow impulses to moral action. . . . One experiences pure spirit by observing, by actually observing how moral forces flow into sense-free thinking." This is something very different from mystical experience, for it is a result of spiritual training, of a sort of scientific discipline through which we discover more organs of knowledge than are available to those who limit themselves, as modern philosophers do, to scientific orthodoxy and to ordinary consciousness. In the last lecture of the present series Steiner speaks of advanced forms of consciousness, of a more acute inner activity, and of higher forms of knowledge.

Contemporary thinkers are often strongly attracted to these higher forms. They approach them enthusiastically, frequently write of them vividly but in the end reject them as retrograde or atavistic, unworthy of a fully accredited modern philosopher.

Paul Valéry, a poet who devoted years of his life to the study of mathematics and who wrote interestingly on Descartes and Pascal, provides us with an excellent example of this in his *Address in Honor of Goethe*. Goethe fascinates Valéry, for Goethe too was a poet who found it necessary to go beyond poetry—"the great apologist of the world of Appearances," Valéry calls him. He says, "I sometimes think that there exists for some people, as there existed for him, an *external life* which has an intensity and a depth at least equal to the intensity and depth that we ascribe to the inner darkness and the mysterious discoveries of the ascetics and the Sufis." Goethe is an investigative and not merely a reactive poet. Valéry greatly admires his botanical work, seeing in it one of "the profound nodal points of his great mind." He goes on to say, "this desire to trace in living things a will to metamorphosis may have been derived from his early contact with certain doctrines, half poetic, half esoteric, which were highly esteemed by the ancients and which, at the end of the eighteenth century, initiates took to cultivating again. The rather seductive if extremely imprecise idea of Orphism, the magical idea of assuming the existence of some unknown hidden principle of life, some tendency towards a higher form of life in every animate and inanimate thing; the idea that a spirit was fermenting in every particle of reality and that it was therefore not impossible to work by the ways of the spirit on everything and every being insofar as it contains a spirit, is among the ideas which bear witness to the persistence of a kind of primitive reasoning and at the same time of an impulse which of its nature generates poetry or personification. Goethe appears to have been deeply imbued with the feeling of this power, which satisfied the poet in him and stimulated the naturalist."

What Valéry assumes here is that there is only one single legitimate method of examining natural phenomena. As a poet he sympathizes with imaginative knowledge, as a thinker he strikes a note of regret and even condolence. "It is one of the clearest examples of transition from poetic thought to scientific theory, or of a fact brought to light by way of a harmony discovered by intuition. Observation verifies what the inner artist has divined. . . . But his great gift of analogy came into conflict with his logical faculties." And the logical faculties, strictly circumscribed, must be obeyed. Magic and primitive reasoning, alas, will not do says the analytical intellect of Valéry.

Steiner had devoted many years of study to Goethe. He was the editor of Goethe's scientific works and in his lectures often refers to him. And there is no nostalgia for "Orphism" in Steiner, no "magic" or "primitive reasoning." He too is a modern thinker. What distinguishes him from most others is his refusal to stop at what he calls "the boundary of the material world." And how does one pass beyond this boundary? By a discipline

that takes us from ordinary consciousness and familiar-
izes us with consciousness of another kind, by finding
the path that leads us into Imagination. "It is possible
to pursue this path in a way consonant with Western
life," he writes, "if we attempt to surrender ourselves
completely to the world of outer phenomena, so that
we allow them to work upon us without thinking about
them, but still perceiving them. In ordinary waking
life, you will agree, we are constantly perceiving, but
actually in the very process of doing so we are continually saturating our percepts with concepts; in scientific
thinking we interweave percepts and concepts entirely
systematically, building up systems of concepts.... One
can become capable of such acute inner activity that
one can exclude and suppress conceptual thinking from
the process of perception and surrender oneself to bare
percepts." This is not a depreciation of thought. Rather,
it releases the imagination. One "acquires a potent psy-
chic force 'when one is able' to absorb the external world
free from concepts." Steiner says, "Man is given over
to the external world continually, from birth onwards.
Nowadays this giving-over of oneself to the external
world is held to be nothing but abstract perception or
abstract cognition. This is not so. We are surrounded by
a world of color, sound and warmth and by all kinds of
sensory impressions." The cosmos communicates with
us also through color, sound and warmth. "Warmth

is something other than warmth; light something
other than light in the physical sense; sound is something other than physical sound. Through our sensory
impressions we are conscious only of what I would term
external sound and external color. And when we surrender ourselves to nature we do not encounter the ether-
waves, atoms and so on of which modern physics and
physiology dream; rather, it is spiritual forces that are
at work, forces that fashion us between birth and death
into what we are as human beings." I have thought it
best not to interpose myself but to allow Steiner to
speak for himself, for he is more than a thinker, he is
an initiate and only he is able to communicate what he
has experienced. The human mind, he tells us, must
learn to will pure thinking, but it must learn also how
to set conceptual thinking aside and to live within the
phenomena. "It is through phenomenology, and not
abstract metaphysics, that we attain knowledge of the
spirit by consciously observing, by raising to consciousness, what we would otherwise do unconsciously; by
observing how through the sense world spiritual forces
enter into our being and work formatively upon it."

We cannot even begin to think of social renewal
until we have considered these questions. What is reality in the civilized West? "A world of outsides without
insides," says Owen Barfield, one of the best interpret-
ers of Steiner. A world of quantities without qualities,

of souls devoid of mobility and of communities which are more dead than alive.

—Saul Bellow

Bibliography

Works mentioned or cited

by Saul Bellow:
The Dean's December
Henderson the Rain King
Humboldt's Gift.
More Die of Heartbreak.
Ravelstein

by Rudolf Steiner:
The Boundaries of Natural Science
The Case for Anthroposophy (Owen Barfield's Introduction)
Cosmic Memory
The Fifth Gospel: From the Akashic Record
Knowledge of the Higher Worlds and Its Attainment
The Philosophy of Spiritual Activity
Spiritual Research: Methods and Results
Speech and Drama
Theosophy
Towards Social Renewal (*The Threefold Commonwealth*)
"The Work of the Angels in Man's Astral Body" (in *Death as Metamorphosis of Life*)

Allan Bloom, *The Closing of the American Mind*

Johann Wolfgang von Goethe, *The Fairytale of the Green Snake and the Beautiful Lily*